PSALMS OF MY LIFE

JOSEPH BAYLY

Victor is an imprint of
Cook Communications Ministries, Colorado Springs, Colorado 80918
Cook Communications, Paris, Ontario
Kingsway Communications, Eastbourne, England

PSALMS OF MY LIFE
© 1987, 2000 by the estate of Joseph Bayly
Printed in Singapore.

Consulting Editor: Timothy B. Bayly
Design: David Carlson Design
Digital imagery © copyright 1999 PhotoDisc, Inc.
Digital imagery © copyright 1999 Digital Stock Corporation

First Printing of 2000 edition
1 2 3 4 5 6 7 8 9 10 Printing/Year 04 03 02 01 00

Library of Congress Cataloging-in-Publication Data

Bayly, Joseph.
     Psalms of my life/Joseph Bayly.
          p.   cm.
     ISBN   1-56476-785-X
     1. Christian poetry, American.   I. Title.
PS3552.A88P7   2000   99-41106
811'.54--dc21   CIP

After graduating from Wheaton College and Faith Theological Seminary, Joe Bayly served as New England regional director with the fledgling InterVarsity Christian Fellowship—followed by terms as editor of *HIS* magazine and director of InterVarsity Press. In 1963 Joe joined David C. Cook Publishing Company where he served in various editorial and management positions.

For twenty-five years Joe wrote a column, "Out of My Mind," for *Eternity* magazine. "Joe wrote with grace and good humor, but he was fearless in confronting evangelicals about questionable practices, false piety, and pompous pretense," said former *Eternity* editor Russell Hitt. Shortly after writing his final column in July 1986, Joe joined three sons who had preceded him in death, leaving behind his wife of forty-three years, Mary Lou, and four children involved in Christian service.

Joe will be remembered as a man of insight and wit, a man keenly sensitive both to the law of God and the weakness of man.

PRAISE *for*
FOUR DAYS

Two days ago
You made the universe
earth sun moon stars
and everything
including man
praise God.
Yesterday
You lived among us
shared our life
taught healed and loved
died for our sins
rose from the dead
praise God.
Today You live in us
who own You Lord
praise God.
Tomorrow You'll return

to claim Your universe
and rule
and every knee
in heaven and earth and under earth
shall bow
and every tongue confess
that You
are Lord
praise God.

A PSALM of PRAISE

Thank You God
that You see
armies march
a sparrow fall
hear
atom's blast
a baby's cry
smell
volcano's flow
a man's sweat
feel
contour of mountains
a little lump
taste
ocean's salt
my tears.

A PSALM of HEIGHTS & DEPTHS

Praise the Lord.
Praise Him in the Rockies
riding mountain trails.
Praise Him
beside tumbling
rushing
rocky
white capped stream.
Praise Him
in high meadow
still forest.
Praise Him on the Cape
eating lobster, clams
walking rainswept beach
barefoot.

Praise Him on Mount Baker
holding ski rope
going uphill
then down.
Praise Him in the snowfall.
Praise Him in the lodge
sitting by the fire
looking out at stars.
Praise Him at the desk
phoning
writing
meeting
planning.
Praise Him in high places
and in low
in excitement
and monotony.
I will sing to the Lord
as long as I live.
I will be glad in the Lord
in the Lord.

BIRTHDAY PSALM

Tonight I'm fifty,
I've lived
for half a century
one twentieth
of a millennium.
One billion
eight hundred thirty-nine million
six hundred thousand
times
my heart has beat.
eighteen thousand
two hundred fifty
times

I've gone to bed,
safe risen in the morning.
For this I thank you,
Lord who forgives,
Lord who heals
my sicknesses
and all my hurts.
Tonight I pray, Lord,
and every night to come
until night ends
and darkness flies away,
remind me of your mercy.

And then tomorrow,
when morning light returns,
and I arise
to love you, serve you,
remind me of your grace.
Listen, angels,
hosts of heaven,
listen servants of the Lord,
celebrate his work in me,
my blessings on his name.

A PSALM *on*
BEING CHILDLIKE

Lord, we're alone
for the first time
in more than three decades
We're alone.
No children home.
I said, "Lord
where is the way?"
You said, "I am
the way."
Lord of childhood
make me childlike
not childish
trusting
not scared
simple
not devious.
When you plow a field
Lord
I know you plan
a crop
when you harrow
breaking up plowed clods of dirt
to fine earth.

A PSALM in
A HOTEL ROOM

I'm alone Lord
alone
a thousand miles from home.
There's no one here who knows
my name
except the clerk
and he spelled it wrong
no one to eat dinner with
laugh at my jokes
listen to my gripes
be happy with me about what
happened today
and say that's great.

No one cares.
There's just this lousy bed
and slush in street outside
between the buildings.
I feel sorry for myself
and I've plenty of reason to.
Maybe I ought to say
I'm on top of it
praise the Lord
things are great
but they're not.
Tonight
it's all
gray slush.

PSALM *of*
THE BATON PASS

Written at a time of being aware
of my midlife crisis

Within my grasp Lord
you've put it there.
It's my turn now
to grip it hard
and run.
But I'm not ready yet
Lord you see
I thought the ones before
would run the race
much longer than they did

far too soon
the baton is mine.
They knew the course
I don't
it's unfamiliar ground
to me.
They knew the way
to pace themselves
I fear that I'll run wild
falter stumble
fall flat
before my race is done,
perhaps begun.
They had the training
of their years
. . . they trained me.
For what?
To run of course
some future day
but not today
not yet.
They've left the field
baton and race are mine

I know it well.
I'm running now
reluctantly.
Hey Lord that's great
you're pacing me
. . . you paced them too?
you're keeping me
from stumbling falling
. . . you kept them too?
The race is hard
and great
I'll never stop
until you take
baton from me
my hard clenched fist
and give it
to the children
of my flesh
of your Spirit.
Look Lord
they're running laps
here
along with us.
Let's run harder.

A PSALM *about* SELF

Lord save me
from myself
my settled self
unsettle me
bring to end of rope
but only
if you
are at the end.
My procrastinating self
that can so easy find
side roads
that are more interesting

even ones where
errands can be run.
Send me back to
my comfort loving self
uncomfort me
pull the covers from me
on cold night
that I may
wake. Starve my body
that my soul may feast.
My proud self.
Give me grace to bend myself
And keep me bent
lest you should one day
bend me to the breaking point.

My righteous self
show me sin
that lurks beneath
my conscious thought
motivating
that pushes me
to settling
comfort pride
and self
rationalizing self
that finds excuse
for what I do
and don't.
Save me from myself
Save me so that
self may die
and save me
from pride
that self is dead.

A Psalm *of* Single Mindedness

Lord of reality
make me real
not plastic
synthetic
pretend phony
an actor playing out his part
hypocrite.
I don't want
to keep a prayer list
but to pray
not agonize to find Your will
but to obey
what I already know
to argue
theories of inspiration
but submit to Your Word.
I don't want
to explain the difference

between eros and philos
and agape
but to love.
I don't want
to sing as if I mean it
I want to mean it.
I don't want
to tell it like it is
but to be it
like You want it.
I don't want
to think another needs me
but I need him
else I'm not complete.
I don't want to tell others how to
do it
but to do it
to have to be always right
but admit it
when I'm wrong.

I don't want
to be a census taker
but an obstetrician
nor an involved person
a professional
but a friend.
I don't want
to be insensitive
but to hurt
where other people hurt
nor to say
I know how you feel
but to say God knows
and I'll try
if you'll be patient with me
and meanwhile I'll be quiet.
I don't want
to scorn the clichés of others
but to mean everything I say
including this.

A PSALM *of* DIGNITY

Thank You
Lord Christ
for treating every other person
as an end
not a means
including me.
Thank You
that You never climbed
on other person's shoulders
never used a man or woman
boy or girl
as if he were a thing.
Thank You
for refusing to invade
the freedom
You have given us.
Thank You for refusing
to manipulate us
pressure us
maneuver us into a corner.
Thank You for treating us
as if we shared Your image.

A PSALM *of* THE FAT CAMEL

This needle's eye
Lord
it is so very small
and I'm so very big
I can't squeeze through
not even little finger.
But then
I'm part of
the affluent society.
We've shown
as never people did before
how to get acquire
build up
squander

and still get more
more things
cars houses
land rosebushes
money
stocks and bonds
more gross national product
and more defenses of it all
more of everything
this side of
needle's eye.
Lord have mercy.
Do a necessary miracle.

A PSALM *of*
FORGETFULNESS

Lord
I'm becoming forgetful
names words
ideas
whether I did this or that.
Remind me Lord
of my memory.
Keep me sharp.
But if it ever
comes to that
let me forget everything
except
Jesus loves me
this I know
for the Bible
tells me so
and others love me
even if I forget
everything
including their names.

A PSALM WHEN
THINGS ARE
GOING WELL

Save me
God
from success.
I fear it
more than failure
which alerts me
to my nature
limitations
destiny.
I know that any success
apart from Your Spirit
is mere euphemism
for failure.

Lord of the compost heap
you take garbage
and turn it into
soil good soil
for seeds to root
and grow
with wildest increase
flowers to bloom
with brilliant beauty.
Take all the garbage
of my life
Lord of the compost heap
turn it into
soil good soil
and then plant seeds
to bring forth
fruit and beauty
in profusion.

A PSALM WHILE
PACKING BOOKS

This cardboard box
Lord
see it says
Bursting limit
200 lbs. per square inch.
The box maker knew
how much strain
the box would take
what weight
would crush it.
You are wiser than the box maker
Maker of my spirit
my mind
my body.
Does the box know
when pressure increases close to
the limit?
No
it knows nothing.
But I know
when my breaking point
is near.
And so I pray
Maker of my soul
Determiner of the pressure
within
upon me
Stop it
lest I be broken
or else
change the pressure rating
of this fragile container
of Your grace
so that I may bear more.

A PSALM
of MEMORIES

Lord
I smell fresh bread
just baked
mouth watering warm.
Lord, my mind goes back
mother kneading dough
taking loaf from pan
buttering a slice for me.
I smell trailing arbutus
sweet breath of mountain
springtime
heavenly fragrance
I remember father
hands extended with arbutus
coming through the door
saying
Mary I found this
for you
in cinders
beside the railroad track
I smell baby powder
and hold again
a tiny infant now grown
our very own
smelling fresh, clean, human
as baby's mother
lifts him from the bath
Hands baby to me
and says, "Hold him, he's ours
our very own."
Lord thank you
for smells
that trigger memory
warm again with love.

A Psalm *of* Minor Miracles

Thank you
for what Deborah
calls minor miracles
Lord
like finding
a paper bag
a clean one

there on the sidewalk
ten steps after
you prayed for it
or going down
that awful
dirt road
on the side of the mountain
and only passing
four cars
in eight miles.

A Psalm *of* Desperation

God
hear my
silent
scream
say
peace
be still
to the storm
that rages
within me.

A Psalm of Suffering

Lord you're the farmer
I'm your field
It is your right
to fence me in
to plow
my soul's hard ground
with furrows deep
to dig down far
for hidden rocks
to harrow hard
till soil is smooth
but only
if you plan
a harvest
of holiness.

A Psalm of Personal Need

Lord, my heart is a ghetto
walled off
dark
depressed
danger filled
hurting.
Move in, Lord.
Renew it
renew my heart
destroy, burn
raze
remove.
Build it fresh
and then You live there.
You Lord.
Because then it'll stay
clean
pure
new.

A P S A L M *o f*
O B S E S S I O N

In times of crisis
Lord
when we don't know
which way
the scales will tip
all else is
unimportant.
We couldn't care less about money
things
about what we eat
or whether.
We don't notice
rebuffs
comments that would ordinarily
disturb us.
Our mind is honed

to single edge.
You loom
above all else
fill our horizon.
Your will
becomes our food
our drink
the very air we breathe.
Too soon
the crisis passes
and we're back
where we were
before.
Dear Lord forgive.

A Psalm *of* Extremity

I cry tears
to you Lord
tears
because I cannot speak.
Words are lost
among my fears
pain
sorrows
losses
hurts
but tears

You understand
my wordless prayer
You hear.
Lord
wipe away my tears
all tears
not in distant day
but now
here.

A PSALM *at*
CHILDREN'S HOSPITAL

I find it hard Lord
agonizing hard
to stand here
looking through the glass
at this my infant son.
What suffering
is in this world
to go through pain of birth
and then through
pain of knife
within the day.
What suffering
is in the world
this never ending
pain parade
from birth
to death.

He moves a bit
not much
how could an infant
stuffed with tubes
cut sewed and bandaged
move more than that?
Some day he'll shout
and run a race
roll down a grassy hill
ice skate
on frosty night like this.
He'll sing and laugh
I know he will Lord.
But if not
if You should take him home
to Your home
help me then remember
how Your Son suffered
and You stood by
watching

agonizing watching
waiting
to bring all suffering to an end
forever
on a day
yet to be.
Look Lord
he sleeps.
I must go now.
Thank You for staying
nearer than oxygen
than dripping plasma
to my son.
Please be that near
to mother
sister brothers
and to me.

A PSALM *on* THE
DEATH OF AN
EIGHTEEN-YEAR-
OLD SON

What waste Lord
this ointment precious
here outpoured
is treasure great
beyond my mind to think.
For years
until this midnight
it was safe
contained
awaiting careful use
now broken
wasted
lost.

The world is poor
so poor it needs each drop
of such a store.
This treasure spent
might feed a multitude
for all their days
and then yield more.
This world is poor?
It's poorer now
the treasure's lost.
I breath its lingering fragrance
soon even that
will cease.
What purpose served?
The act is void of reason
sense
Lord
madmen do such deeds
not sane.

The sane man hoards his treasure
spends with care
if good
to feed the poor
or else to feed himself.
Let me alone Lord
You've taken from me
what I'd give Your world.
I cannot see such waste
that You should take
what poor men need.
You have a heaven
full of treasure
could You not wait
to exercise Your claim
on this?

O spare me Lord forgive
that I may see
beyond this world
beyond myself
Your sovereign plan
or seeing not
may trust You
Spoiler of my treasure.
Have mercy Lord
here is my quitclaim.

*This poem laments the death of Joe
and Mary Lou Bayly's eldest son,
Joseph Tate Bayly V, who died on
January 19, 1964. He was the
third Bayly child to die. "Passover
Eve, 1964" is a slightly different
version of this same poem, and it was
originally published in the April,
1964 issue of* Eternity *magazine.)*

A PSALM *about* SERIOUS ILLNESS

Thank you Lord Jesus
that you're not embarrassed
by serious illness
serious sin.
You don't draw back
afraid to speak
lest you say the wrong thing
afraid to touch
lest you become unclean tainted
too involved.
Thank you
that you bore these sins
these sicknesses and sorrows
you entered into
serious illness serious sin.

A PSALM *in* A HOSPITAL CORRIDOR

Lord
my heart fears.
I know that You have said
Fear not
but my heart fears.
Thoughts flash
across the track of my mind
thoughts of evil
not good
loss
not gain
suffering
not joy.
My thoughts are out of control.

They exhume the past
bury the future
make the present
a heavy heavy burden.
Lord
I cannot control
these fears these thoughts.
I cannot look at the future
with peace.
But I trust You.
These fears run wild
careering thoughts of evil
may make it seem
that I don't
but I do.
I trust You Lord.
I know Your thoughts toward me
are of good
not evil.
I fear evil
not You.

Yet fearing wild
I know that even evil
from Your hand
is purest good.
I fear
I trust.
I trust You Lord
I trust Your wisdom
life spanning
Your love
death taming.
I trust You
to know the end of this long
beginning
moment.

A Psalm *of* Awakening

Lord I want to die
in my sleep
I want to go to bed
and be awakened
by you
saying
Get up son
it's the first day of school
the beginning of your new job
the dawn of eternity.
Here are your clothes.
Your older brother
wore them first
now they're yours
forever
white and fresh and clean
smelling of heaven.

A PSALM *on* BEING

The little child says
Here I am daddy
as he bursts
on father's sight
from behind the chair
where he's been hiding.
He doesn't say
What can I do for you?
How can I help you?
I want to serve you
seeking somehow
to work and gain
the father's favor
and delight.
He knows that they are his
without exhausting effort
to achieve.
They are his always.
Here I am daddy
—Abba Father—
not working
just being your eternal son.

A PSALM *on* VIEWING THE RIVER

Lord
if anything happens
if you come for me
keep them from interfering
desperately trying
to tug me
from your grasp.
If I'm far
across the river
where you own shore
and all beyond
don't let them
bring me back
prolonging death
not life
delaying life
that never crosses
unreturning river
again.

A PSALM *for* CHRISTMAS EVE

Praise God for Christmas
Praise Him for the Incarnation
for Word made flesh.
I will not sing
of shepherds watching flocks
on frosty night
or angel choristers.
I will not sing
of stable bare in Bethlehem
or lowing oxen
wise men
trailing distant star
with gold and frankincense and
myrrh.

Tonight I will sing
praise to the Father
who stood on heaven's threshold
and said farewell to His Son
as He stepped across the stars
to Bethlehem
and Jerusalem.
And I will sing
praise to the infinite eternal Son
who became most finite
a Baby
who would one day be executed
for my crimes.
Praise Him in the heavens.
Praise Him in the stable.
Praise Him in my heart.

A P S A L M *of*
            C H R I S T M A S

Lord we blame
the innkeeper
for only giving you
the stable
when his inn was full
but what about
all the others
who lived in Bethlehem
that night
when you were born.
Why were
all their houses
that weren't full
of guests
fast closed
against the one
who contained you?

God bless
our little homes
this Christmastime
make them
big enough
to welcome you
contained in those
for whom the world
has no room
except
a cold and lonely
Christmas day.

A PSALM *for*
PALM SUNDAY

King Jesus
why did you choose
a lowly ass
to carry you
to ride in your parade?
Had you no friend
who owned a horse
—a royal mount with spirit
fit for a king to ride?
Why choose an ass
small unassuming
beast of burden
trained to plow
not carry kings.

King Jesus
why did you choose
me
a lowly unimportant person
to bear you
in my world today?
I'm poor and unimportant
trained to work
not carry kings
—let alone the King of kings
and yet you've chosen me
to carry you in triumph
in this world's parade.
King Jesus
Keep me small
so all may see
how great you are
keep me humble
so all may say
Blessed is he who cometh in the
name of the Lord
not what a great ass he rides.

Tonight
Lord Jesus Christ
You sat at supper
with Your friends.
It was a simple meal
that final one
of lamb
unleavened bread
and wine.
Afterward
You went out to die.

How many other meals You
shared
beside the lake
fried fish and toasted bread
at Simon's banquet hall a feast
at Lazarus' home in Bethany
the meal that Martha cooked
on mountain slope
where You fed hungry crowd
at close of tiring day.
Please sit with us tonight
at our small meal
of soup and rolls and tea.
Then go with us
to feast of bread and wine
that You provide
because afterward
You went out to die.

PASSOVER EVE,
1964

What waste!

This ointment, precious,
here outpoured,
Is treasure great beyond
our minds to think.
For years, until this
moment, it was safe,
Contained, awaiting
careful use.
Now broken, wasted, lost.
The world is poor.

So poor it needs each drop of
such a store.
This treasure sold might
feed a multitude
For all their days.
This world is poor?
It's poorer now
The treasure's lost.
Breathe deep
Its fragrance; soon even
that will cease,
Except perhaps on hands
that poured it out.
What purpose served?

The act is void of reason,
    sense,
    Madmen do such deeds,
    not sane.
    Sane men hoard their
    treasure, spend with care:
    If good, to feed the poor;
    or else
    To feed themselves.

Let her alone.
    She gives to me what you
    would give the world.
    You cannot understand
    such waste,
    She wonders that at such a
    time you'd choose
    The poor. Her guilt not
    waste, but love.
    She knows the value, you
    the cost,
    Of treasure she possessed,
    not you;
    And poured out on my
    head, my feet,
    Against tomorrow, when
    I die, and next day
    Fragrance fresh, renewed.

A Psalm *for* Easter

Let's celebrate Easter
with the rite
of laughter.
Christ died and rose
and lives.
Laugh like a woman
who holds her first baby.
Our enemy death
will soon be destroyed.
Laugh like a man
who finds he doesn't have cancer
or does but now there's a cure.
Christ opened wide the door of
heaven.

Laugh like children
at Disneyland's gates.
This world is owned by God
and He'll return to rule.
Laugh like a man
who walks away uninjured
from a wreck
in which his car was totaled.
Laugh
as if all the people in the whole
world
were invited to a picnic
and then invite them.

A P s a l m *of*
          P r e a c h i n g

I'm on the bridge
Lord
the ship's bridge
steering shipload
of your people. There they are
on the deck looking up
trusting
scarcely knowing
of the icebergs
hidden reefs
wrecks of long gone ships
that I'm avoiding.
Keep me glued
to chart

that you've provided
to Holy Spirit's course
sensing dangers
most of all
the danger that I'll think
beyond the steering
I provide
power to make the ship move
on its appointed course.
Bring us all
to safe harbor
by twelve o'clock.

A PSALM of APPRECIATION FOR THE NEW CHURCH

This pew
is soft
cushioned.
Thank You Lord
for our new sanctuary
acoustically
near perfect
so we can hear
no matter how deaf
lighting
by an illumination engineer
so we can see with even dimmest
sight
air conditioned
so we can shut out
the heat
be cool
no matter what.

It's a great new sanctuary.
This soft pew
cushions me
against the wood.

A PSALM on MOVING TO TAKE A NEW JOB

I take this step
Lord
in faith.
Faith You
have confronted me
with this opening
Faith that You
have led me to accept

Faith that this change
will be a means
to great holiness
and love
to You
for me
my wife
our children
Faith
that You will make me
able for this new work
so that I may add
in every way
to what You
are already doing
where I go
Faith
that You will care
for mother sister
friends needy ones
we leave behind

Faith that You will make me
creative in my work
and in the exercise
of other gifts
Faith that by this change
You will make
life and self we share
my wife's and mine
and ours together
more real
more full
than it has been to now
Faith that this change
will bring much blessing
to each of our children
Faith in Your promise
that when You put forth
Your own sheep
You go before them.
Lord I will not go
unless You do this.

A PSALM *on*
SPOTTING
   SPUTNIK 1957

See that speck
Lord
we put it there.
Not really us Lord
the Russians did.
It shines so bright
as it passes
over Memorial Field
through darkling sky.
It is our evensong.
Whose sun does it reflect?
Why Yours
Lord.
Sputnik
is ours
the sun belongs to You.

A PSALM *of*
   CHURCH BUILDING

Let me build a church Lord
That's big enough for You.
Not big enough for them
or him or her
or me
but You.
Red door
open wide
high walls
enough to hem us in
to You
Your mind
windows without glass
through which
dove may fly
steeple
rising rising
through low clouds
to sky
and star beyond
tolling death
pealing life.

A Psalm *of* Appreciation for Music

Thank You for music
Lord
Handel and Haydn Society
and Boston Symphony
present
Handel's Messiah.
He shall feed His flock
like a shepherd
shall gather the lambs with His
arm
and carry them in His bosom.
Students on Fairview Island
singing
Who is on the Lord's side
who will serve the King?

Mother holding little boy
rocking
humming
All through the night
my Savior will be watching
and Like a river glorious
is God's perfect peace.
Little group of people
before an open grave
singing
Jesus I love Thee
and up from the grave He arose.

A P s a l m *on*
T W A F l i g h t 8 1

High above the clouds
six miles over earth
I think of Time
and Life
not timeless life
or coffee tea or milk
not living water
bread of life
of landing
on hard concrete strip
not flying on
to meet You.
I guess I fear that.
Earthbound in the heavens
Lord
not heavenbound.
Lord have mercy.

A P s a l m *of*
T h a n k s g i v i n g
f o r a C h r i s t i a n
B o o k s t o r e

Thank you, Lord
for this store
where bread is sold
to feed the soul.
Not stones
that after they have failed
to quiet hunger
break the teeth
or serpents
that pretend to satisfy
the frightful lust
of one who eats
and then
administer
the sting of death.

But bread from heaven
via Bethlehem
that House of Bread
where one night's toil
produced enough
to feed a starving world
of souls
through all of time
and via Calvary
where bread was broken
to arise afresh
and fill the world
with warm aroma
of loaf
fresh baked
life giving
death halting.

Can any store
put out this bread
for sale?
No, bread of life
is without price
and anyone who hungers
has it free.
Containers only
are for sale
to take it home
and eat
or feed another.

Thank you Lord
for this store
where bread is sold
to feed the soul.

A Psalm *in* a
Colorado
Meadow

Twenty wild flowers Lord
no twenty-two.
Here they are
all round where I sit
waiting.

I don't know their names
except arbutus
trailing arbutus
and daisies.
Maybe I could give names
to the rest.

Blue glory in the morning
or blue funk
yellow elf
Aunt Elizabeth's prayerbook
Job's tears
there are a lot of them Lord
all over the meadow.
Lonely gumdrop
the purple kind
that's left in the dish
when all the rest are gone.
Mouse corsage
gopher's hay.

Pink pumps of pinkelumps
Sergeant Pepper's epaulets
Eleanor Rigby's shroud.
Let's see
did I name that one
or those?
I've lost track.
The rest will be nameless
because here come the children
running through the stream
back from climbing
their stone mountain.
Thank You for wild flowers
Lord
mountains
rushing streams
children
each different.
Thank You.

A Psalm of
St. Elmo Colorado

This ghost town
Lord
once live
now dead
boarded up
against the world
the flesh
the devil.
The devil? No
he lives here
in shuttered house
abandoned mine
boarded post office
tavern store.
He's at home
in ghost town
not town alive
with children
hammers
violins.

A Psalm of
Bear Trap
Revisited in
the Fall

Lord, I see the aspen
stand out gold
among the green and gray
of mountains round.
It takes the fall
to isolate them
set them stark
defined
they can
no longer hide.
Twenty summers ago
Lord
We planted trees
here
in Brown Bear
Pooh Bear

Three Bears Polar Bear
Lodge
Cook House
Bear's Den
and this log
on sunny afternoon
here
where I sit.
Now fall has come
and some stand
tall and gold
amid encircling pines.

Others are small
too short to see
distinguish from
the gray and green
A few though still alive have died
while other few
alive
though dead
have grown beyond
the mountains
mist
and sky.
You cannot hide
an aspen
planted on
rocky mountain
when fall comes.
I wonder about the trees
they're planting
summers now.

A Psalm in
Mojave Desert

I said
this desert land is barren
void of life and beauty.
I drive for miles
see nothing
only sand and sage
feel nothing
only wind and heat
taste nothing
but spit dried spit.

He said
have you ever driven
in spring
though this same desert
seen blossoms flower
gorgeous wild?
It's all a thing of timing.
Seeds of beauty
are there now hidden
waiting fall of rain
to bring them life.
Lord send rain
upon my world
my life
I'm tired of dried spit.

A Psalm *of* Meaning Exchange

I will praise the Lord
for communications media.
For printed page
that says
a hundred thousand times
God loves you.
Here's the answer
to your problem
question doubt need.
For radio broadcast
television program
that enters in
where doors are closed
blinds drawn
homes without number
cars
hospital wards
prison cells
barracks

dormitory rooms
and says
You're not alone.
God loves you.
He'll meet you here
and now.
You needn't go out
to strange church
crowded meeting hall.
For records tapes
Braille books
that tell the blind
God loves you.
I will praise the Lord

for communications media.
I will praise the Lord
for a man
a woman
who grasps trembling hand
under oxygen tent
who sits on edge
of barracks bed
who looks the prisoner
in the eye

who buys a Coke for student
who walks with blind
and says
God loves you
and they know
he does
too.

A PSALM of
THANKSGIVING
FOR LEADERS

Thank You for our leaders
for pastors
who feed us
serve us and our children
as Your ministers
Son of God
who came not to be served
but to serve
for theologians
who give us answers
questions
reasons for our hope
from Your Word

Father of Lights
for evangelists
who harvest the field
You have brought
to fruition
Holy Spirit
for teachers
who make us think
of You
ourselves and others
because You have taught them.
Thank You for our leaders
Your followers.

A Psalm *in*
          Celebration of
Missionaries

How happy are those
who take the Gospel
to other lands.
They obey Your command
Lord Jesus
Your command to tell
the Good News
everywhere
to every person
in the whole world.
They forsake
kindred and friends
houses and land
comfort security things
to go tell

teach
heal
love
They are the great ones
of this generation
of whom the world
is not worthy.
They are the ones
whom the world pities.
Poor world.
Poor pitiful world.
They are Your ambassadors
sent by You
to declare an end
to hostility
and announce peace
through Your death
and endless life.
How happy are those
who take the Gospel
to other lands.

A PSALM *of*
THE YOUNG PASTOR

Lord
the grass is dry
brown drying
Send rain I ask
refreshing, renewing
reviving rain
an all day rain
that gets down to its roots
so that it will live
again
be green
cool to my feet
Lord
my soul is dry
send rain
down to my roots
so that I may be cool
to your feet

A Psalm *of* a
Weary Prophet

Lord, I'm a weary prophet
You're a prophet?
Even that word
using it for myself
shows my weary state.
You're no Jeremiah
—forgive me
for inveighing like one.
Nor Jonah
—except in the belly
of the great fish.
Nor Amos
—I'm the one
to whom that man spoke.
Maybe I'm just
a common scold
iconoclast
(that sounds better)
critic
controversialist
prophet
—there
I said it again
Who am I
to question
doctrine
manners morals
A voice.
Then let others speak
You'll never be a prophet
but you can speak for me
—like Balaam's ass.

A Psalm *of* Praise for the Tribes

I will sing
of the tribes of earth
who have turned
from darkness
to light
not flickering dying campfire
but sun of opening day.
Walamo
Kambatta Hadiya
Yoruba
Mixtec Tzeltal Cakchiquel
Shapras Aucas
Lisu Katu
Picts
Angles Saxons Swabians
Visigoths.
I will sing
of men and women
who brought light
to the tribes.

Ohman Bergsten
Crouch
Pike Slocum Townsend
Cox and Anderson
The five who died
Elisabeth Elliot
Rachel Saint
Fraser
Smith
Boniface Willibrand
Ulfilas.
I will sing
of the Light
of earth's tribes
who will shine in them
forever.

A Psalm of a Seminary Wife

Books I hate you
hate your claims
upon my husband
hiding there behind your covers
instead of under mine.
Who ever thought that I'd play
second fiddle
to a book?

Typewriter I hate you
typing papers
typing thesis
footnotes, quotes
diaphoresis.
Who ever thought that I'd be
secretary
to my mate?

Apartment I hate you
hate the room
where babies
and cries
disturbing
other tenants
and my husband
as he studies all the time.

Meals I hate you
hate the pennies
I am watching
as I serve
by light of candle
gourmet macaroni dishes
to my educated husband
on the run.

Job I hate you
hate the way
my husband's growing

in his knowledge and becoming
educated more and more
while I'm tied to
stupid repetitions
rote of work.

Husband I hate you
hate your easy
expectation
that I'm free from all emotion
keeping children
from commotion
so that you
can study all the time.

Tears I hate you
hate the way
you come unbidden
when he fails
to hug or kiss me
and when he forgets
to pray or read the Bible
unassigned.

God I love you.
Are you surprised
I know I'd be
if someone griped of situation
thought I'd planned their
deprivation
when my plan
by love conceived
was for their total good.

A PSALM
for A NURSE

Father
I'm a nurse
and patients are enough
to keep me busy
every hour of my day
or night.
But that's not all.
There are the relatives beside
and doctors
orderlies and aides
other nurses too
the chaplain
with all kinds and shapes
of clergymen
and topping all the heap
director and administrator
who run the hospital itself
and me.
Father
I am weak
but others lean on me
I am tired
but others need my strength
I'm alone
full conscious of my solitary life
yet thrust into the hurting circles
of families facing loss.
Father make me competent
a nurse who knows just what to do
in an emergency
at three A.M.
when no one is around
but me.
I want to be a good nurse
the sort that parents trust

with infant treasure
in neonatal care
when they must leave at night.
The sort that senses pain
or fear of pain,
or fear of loss
—of breast of sight
of life itself—
and sensing
shares the word or touch
that turns them from their fears
to you.
Father make me real
a person helping others
without power sick dying
but values far beyond
the hospital itself.
Make me real
not empty uniform
that moves from room to room,
mechanical and cold.

I need your warmth
your love for people
yes for those
who argue in the E.R.
beside the still cold body of their son
about responsibility
for accident for overdose that killed.
I need your warmth
in operating room
toward doctor as he curses
at my clumsiness
my inability to read his mind.
I need your warmth
toward patients who complain
who signal for attention all the
time especially the ones
who aren't as sick

as some who never ask for help.
I need your peace
when face to face with death
unable to do more than hold a hand
and watch.
I feel so helpless
many times.
What good is all my skill
before this awful foe?
I need your balance
lest I become obsessed with death
disease and pain
and think the whole world's sick
including me.
How easily I diagnose
the symptoms of my illness
doubtless fatal.

Help me to turn from pain's parade
to joyful life
from sickness to the world of health
from charts and sterile tubes and
medicines
to family and friends
to bundled children
playing in the snow
without guilt
that I am well
that I can run and see my breath
and eat a dinner out
with candles
and the one I love.

A PSALM *on* A COLD NIGHT

Lord thank you
for this warm presence
here lying at my side
in holy dark.
Thank you
for beauty
present from the start
refined by sufferings
and joys
of forty years.
Thank you
for pureness, patience
faith and courage
love
that mounted
in crescendo
drums and cymbals
now muted quiet
flute and strings
and tiny bells.
Thank you
that turning over

I am warmed
and comforted
by this long burning fire.
She grasps my hand
and squeezes in her sleep.
Tonight Lord
thank you
for that wonder
that what you joined together
no woman man
or hell itself
could sunder.

A PSALM *of* LOVE

Thank you for children
brought into being
because we loved.
God of love
Keep us loving
so that they
may grow up whole
in love's overflow.

A P s a l m _of_ M y s t e r y

You made known Your ways
to Moses God
Your acts
to his people Israel.
They only saw
the sea divide
and swallow Pharaoh's host
the fire by night
the cloud by day.
They tasted manna
quail
drank water from the rock.
It was enough
for them to live
by what You did
leave reason to another.
Not Moses
he was a different sort
who prayed

A P s a l m _of_
P o v e r t y

Lord Christ
You loved the poor.
It was a sign
that You were who
You claimed to be.
You bothered
with them
preached to them
invited to be rich and full.
forgive me Lord
for falling short
of such a love as Yours
that broke through crust
of poverty
for beggar
like me.

Show me now
Your ways O God.
And You did.
You let him see
the principles
behind Your acts
and past the principles
the character displayed
eternal character
that forms the principles
the acts
and all.
Make me a Moses
God
dissatisfied with all things
short of You.

A PSALM *about* THE
SHORTNESS OF LIFE

I said
O Lord
let me end the work
You gave to me to do.
So much
must yet be done
before the dark
so little time
remains
before I'm home.
You are eternal
God
a thousand years to You
is but a passing day.
You scatter ages
I hoard my hours.

Please understand
my need for time
to do Your will
complete my job.
I understand
He said
I do
I only had
three years
of days
and I was through.

A PSALM *of* FAITH

Thunder
crashing roaring
wakens me.
I get up
to close the window
against the rain.
Lightning tears the sky
for fragmentary moment
I see the yard
wheelbarrow
trees road field
and distant hill.
All is dark again
I return to sleep.
Thank You for the storm
that wakens me
and lightning flash
illumining
things near and far
in usual dark.

A P S A L M
   R E Q U E S T I N G   F A I T H

Give me courage Lord
to take risks
not the usual ones
respected
necessary
relatively safe
but those I could avoid
the go for broke ones.
I need courage
not just because
I may fall on my face
or worse
but others seeing me
a sorry spectacle
if it should happen
will say

he didn't know what he was doing
or he's foolhardy
or he's old enough to know
you lead from the side
instead of letting yourself be
caught
in wild stampede.
Give me courage Lord
to take unnecessary risks
live at tension
instead of opting out.
Give me the guts to put up
instead of shutting up.
When it comes right down to it
Lord
I choose to be Your failure
before anyone else's success.
Keep me from reneging
on my choice.

A Psalm *of* Forgiveness

I plead guilty
Lord
I stand
awaiting
sentence
my crimes
spread out before You
Just judge
of all the earth
I have no words
to lessen guilt.
No other can I blame
distant Adam
near people
except myself.

My guilt I bear
alone.
Alone?
Another stood alone
before You
and took my sentence
Lord.
Now I am free
to praise you
Just Judge
to please you
Criminal in my place.

A PSALM *to*
THE GOD MAN

Lord Jesus Christ
I thank you
that you were real
a real man
and before that
a real boy.
It hurt
when you were planing wood
and you got a splinter
under your nail.
You felt it
when a stone got stuck
in your sandal.
You had to shake it out.
You removed the sand
from between your toes
and slept on hard ground

on cold night
dreaming of foxes
with their warm holes.
You got thirsty
hungry
tired
bone tired
tired of crowds
tired because you walked
too far.
You died.
Lord Jesus Christ
I thank you
that you were real
real God.
You healed people's hurts
even raised their dead.
You said

Come to me
if you're tired
and I will give you rest.
You fed hungry crowds
and said
I am living bread
that came down from heaven.
You rose from deadness
into life bringing life.
Lord Jesus Christ
I thank you
that you were real
real God man.
I worship you
I adore you
because you who bore
my sins
know what it's like
to have a splinter
under your nail
and to die.

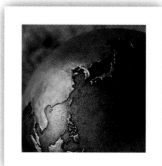

A PSALM *of*
    WORLD AND LIFE

Lord give me a view
of this world
and this life
the sort that comes
when you climb a mountain
a hill
or even go out
on a rooftop.
I want to see things from above
from your perspective
not from beneath.

I want to see
you at work
in history including
the evening news
nature's beauty
nature's terror
science space
the church in history
and today.
I want to see
your image
shine through music, art,
drama, books.
But most of all
let me view
my life
from above
see goals, priorities,
achievements, failures
from your perspective.
O Lord
burn eternity
into my eyeballs.

A PSALM *of* TODAY

This is the day
the Lord has made.
The Lord?
Today?
Yesterday perhaps
could claim Your craft
or hopefully tomorrow
but not today
this disappointing day so filled
with problems
needs
despair and doubt.
This is the day
the Lord has made
and making it
He'll give me strength
and hope
to take me through.
This is the day
the Lord has made
so I'll be glad
and I'll rejoice in it.

A PSALM *of*
WANDERING

Lord You know
I'm such a stupid sheep.
I worry
about all sorts of things
whether I'll find grazing land
still cool water
a fold at night
in which I can feel safe.
I don't.

I only find troubles
want
loss.
I turn aside from You
to plan my rebel way.
I go astray.
I follow other shepherds
even other stupid sheep
Then when I end up
on some dark mountain
cliffs before
wild animals behind
I start to bleat
Shepherd Shepherd
find me save me
or I die.
And You do.

A PSALM *of*
ASSURANCE

I said
Lord give me assurance
that I'm really saved.
I find doubt
uncertainty
so easy
I want to feel
consistently
I'm justified
just as if I'd never sinned
pardoned
sure of gaining heaven.

He said
Isn't my word
enough?
I've promised
you will never perish
you're held in my hand
and in my father's hand.
Can life eternal
ever end?
Will any father
desert
child he loves?
Yes some would
but would I
loving you with
everlasting love?

When birth comes
from above
can you go back
into the womb?
why seek more
believe less
than I have promised?
I shall never leave you
nor forsake you.
will I ever abandon
the sheep I found
and brought back
to the fold?

Lord Christ
Your servant
Martin Luther
said he only had
two days
on his calendar
today
and that day
and that's
what I want too.
and I want
to live
today
for
that day.

*Finally, a poem Joe Bayly lovingly inscribed on
the back of a Mother's Day card to his dear wife,
Mary Lou, shortly before his death.*

TO M.L.
        MOTHER'S DAY,
1982

—to celebrate your creation
of children
What a Holy Spirit calling:
To create an infant
within yourself
Your very inmost self—
Nourish, protect, prepare
Then bring to birth
Nurse, feed
—run between stove and table in
teenage—

Teach, discipline, hope, expect
Love
And all the while pray
with faith in God
Bring to safe harbor
through calm and storm
and monstrous waves
to wholeness
and useful life
on earth
in heaven
    That God should call
    three to live and serve there
    four to live and serve here
What a calling!

Your Joe